LOUIS BRAILLE

The boy who invented books for the blind

Louis Braille

the boy who invented books for the blind

by MARGARET DAVIDSON

Illustrated by Janet Compere

HASTINGS HOUSE, PUBLISHERS

New York

Fourth Printing, September 1979
Text copyright © 1971 by Margaret Davidson.
Ilustrations © 1971 by Janet Compere.
This edition published 1972 by Hastings House Publishers, Inc.
by arrangement with Scholastic Book Services,
a division of Scholastic Magazines, Inc., original publishers
of the softcover edition of the book.

   ❀   ❀   ❀

   ❀   ❀   ❀

Published simultaneously in Canada by
Saunders of Toronto, Ltd., Don Mills, Ontario

Library of Congress Cataloging in Publication Data
Davidson, Mickie
    Louis Braille, the boy who invented books for the
blind.
    SUMMARY: The life of the nineteenth-century French-
man who invented an alphabet enabling the blind to
read.
    1. Braille, Louis, 1809-1852—Juvenile literature.
[1. Braille, Louis, 1809-1852. 2. Blind]
I. Compere, Janet, illus. II. Title.
HV1624.B65D37   371.9′11′0924   [B]   [92]   73-39630
ISBN 0-8038-4281-3

Library of Congress Catalog Card Number 73-39630
Printed in the United States of America .

CONTENTS

LOUIS BRAILLE

The boy who invented books for the blind

Louis Braille

L ouis sat on the front stoop of his house. It was a fine spring morning and all around him things were happening. Fluffy clouds were sailing across a bright blue sky. A bird was building a nest in a nearby tree. A cow was grazing in the next field. A rabbit hopped by. A bug inched across a leaf. All around things were happening. But Louis didn't see any of it. Five-year-old Louis Braille was blind in both eyes.

It hadn't always been this way. Once Louis had been able to see as well as anyone else. For the first three years of his life he had been able to see trees and fields and the river and sky. He had been able to see the streets and buildings of Coupvray, the little town in France where he lived. He had been able to see his father and mother, his brother and sisters, and the small stone cottage where they lived. But one day all that changed.

Louis's father was a harness maker. "The best in all of France," he liked to say. Men came from miles around to have Simon Braille make harnesses and saddles for their horses.

Louis liked to listen to the men talk and joke and laugh. But he liked it best when they left. Then his father put on his big leather apron and went to work.

Louis was too young to help. But he loved to watch his father work. He was only three years old. But already he knew what he wanted to be when he grew up — a harness maker, just like his father!

By the side of Simon Braille's workbench were fat rolls of leather. Hanging on the wall behind were neat rows of tools. There were tools to twist and tools to tighten. Tools to cut and tools to punch holes. Knives, mallets, punches, awls — Louis knew the names of them all. How he longed to hold them in his hands just once.

"They are too sharp," his father said. "Too dangerous for a little boy's hands. Do you understand, Louis?"

Louis's eyes grew big. His father's voice was so stern. "Yes, Papa," he said.

"Then *promise.*"

"I promise."

But sometimes promises are hard to keep. One hot summer day Louis was wandering around in front of the house. He couldn't think of a thing to do. And everyone was busy. Too busy to bother with him.

Of course he could play by himself. But he didn't *feel* like playing by himself. So he tried to help his mother in the garden for a while. Louis thought he was pulling up weeds. But it wasn't always easy for three-year-old Louis to tell weeds from other growing things.

"Oh, Louis!" his mother cried. "That's the

third carrot you've pulled up in a row. Thank you for helping, dear. Now why don't you go help someone else?"

But everyone else was busy too. So Louis stood in front of his father's workshop — growing more and more bored. He took a deep breath. The smell of leather was very strong. He peered into the crowded workshop room. In the corner he saw his father's bench. Louis wandered inside.

He moved closer and closer to the bench. And there right in the middle of it was a long piece of leather. Next to the leather was an awl — a long, pointed tool for punching holes. Louis knew he shouldn't. But he did it anyway. He picked up the awl and began to dig it into the leather.

The leather was slippery. And so was the

awl. Suddenly the awl skidded. It seemed to jump through the air — and plunged right into Louis's eye!

Louis screamed! His mother came running. She held him close and bathed his eye. The doctor came as fast as he could. But Louis's eye had been terribly hurt.

Soon it became infected. Louis rubbed and rubbed at it with his hands. Before long the infection spread to his other eye. Then it seemed to Louis as if a gray curtain had fallen in front of his face. At first he could still see. But not very clearly. As time passed he saw less and less. Until one day Louis could barely see light coming in through the window. The next day he could not even see the sun.

Louis was too young to understand what had happened to him. "When will morning come?" he asked again and again. How everyone hated that question! For by now they all knew that the answer was "never" for Louis Braille. He would be blind for the rest of his life.

Blind Boy

TODAY blind children go to school. They learn how to read and write. They can do many things other children do. When they grow up they can work at many different jobs.

This was not always so. When Louis was a boy in the early 1800's, blind children almost never went to school. They did not learn to read or write — or much of anything else. And life got no better when they grew up. There were so few things for blind people to do. Some worked like horses or oxen pulling heavy loads. Some shoveled coal in factories. But most became beggars.

There were many blind beggars in Louis's day. They stood on city street corners. They wandered the roads of the land. They dressed in rags. They slept in dark alleys or on the hard stone steps of a church. Sometimes they managed to beg enough money for a meal. But often they ate garbage like stray dogs. Or they went hungry — and hoped for a better day tomorrow.

The town of Coupvray was not a big place. But it had a blind beggar too. One day he just wandered into town. No one knew from where. One day he would be gone. And no one would care.

This must not happen to their son. The Brailles were going to make sure of that! They wanted Louis to have a good and happy life — as happy as possible.

At first it wasn't easy. Poor Louis. His life had been turned topsy-turvy. At first he bumped into everything. Again and again his family wanted to cry "Watch out!" "Be careful!" "Stop!" But most of the time they didn't. They hated to see Louis hurt himself.

But they wanted him to learn how to get around by himself. They didn't want him to grow up as so many blind children did — scared to do anything.

It would have been easy to spoil Louis. Everyone felt so sorry for him. But Louis's mother and father wanted him to be as much like other people as possible. So they treated him as much like other people as possible.

Louis was blind, but he still had chores to do. Simon Braille taught him how to polish leather with wax and a soft cloth. Louis could not see the leather growing shiny. But he could feel it getting smoother and smoother — until his fingers told him the job was done.

Simon also taught his son to weave leather fringes. These gay-colored fringes would hang as decorations from finished harnesses.

Louis also helped his mother around the house. Every evening he helped her set the table for dinner. He knew just where to put each cup and plate and bowl. Every morning he went to the well to fill a bucket with drinking water. The bucket was heavy. And the path was rocky. Sometimes Louis stumbled and the water spilled. But he knew there could be no excuses. He knew he had to go back and get some more.

Then Simon Braille cut his son a long pointed-tipped cane. That helped. Louis learned to sweep the cane in front of him as he walked. When it hit something, he knew it was time to stop and turn aside.

Sometimes Louis could tell he was going to bump into something — a wall, a fence, a door — without using his cane at all. He did it by singing a tune. "When I sing I can see my way much better," he liked to say.

Of course he couldn't really *see*. He was doing what bats have always done. Bats can hardly see at all. But they can fly around in the darkest caves without bumping into anything. They do it by sound. They make a high squeaking sound as they fly. The sound travels ahead of them until it bumps into something hard — like the wall of a cave. Then the faintest *echo* of this sound comes bouncing back. When the bats hear this tiny sound they know it is time to turn away. Now Louis was learning to do this too.

Louis was learning more and more things. And he was growing more sure of himself. Soon the sound of his cane — *tap, tap, tap* — was heard everywhere in the cobblestone streets of Coupvray. Sometimes he got lost. But this happened less and less often. Louis was learning to live by clues.

He knew when he was near the bakery by the heat of the ovens — and the spicy-sweet smells. Louis could tell all sorts of things by their shapes and the different ways they felt. But the sounds of the world were most important of all.

The *bong, bonggg, bonggGG* of the old

village church bell, a neighbor's dog barking, a blackbird calling from a nearby tree, the gurgle of the brook. They told him where he was — and what was going on.

Louis liked especially to sit on the front stoop of his house and call out to the people passing by on the road. He almost never made a mistake. How could he tell so many different people apart? he was often asked. "It's so easy," he always said.

After all, a two-wheel cart sounded very different from a four-wheel wagon. And the fast clip-clop of a team of horses sounded different from the slow plod-plod of a yoke of oxen.

People sounded different too. One man had a deep cough. Another had the habit of whistling through his teeth. A third man walked with a limp. "Don't you see?" Louis felt like saying. "There are so many ways to tell people apart — if only you listen!"

A Special Friend

B UT sometimes Louis listened — and heard things he didn't want to hear. Sometimes he would overhear someone say, "There goes poor Louis Braille. Isn't it a pity!"

Louis hated talk like this! He didn't feel poor — not in any way! But he did know he was different. And as Louis grew older this got harder and harder to bear.

There were so many things he couldn't do. He couldn't play tag or hide-and-seek. He couldn't run down the road to a friend's house. Or creep with the other boys through the woods to a secret hide-out.

Everyone in town liked Louis. But this

wasn't the same as having a best friend, or belonging to a gang.

Louis had always laughed and talked a lot. Now, more and more often, he sat sad and silent. "What are you *thinking*?" his parents asked again and again. "Nothing," Louis usually answered.

But when Louis was six years old a new priest came to the village church of Coupvray — Father Jacques Palluy. And Father Palluy was going to change Louis's life in many ways.

Father Palluy wanted to get to know the people of his church as fast as possible. So he went visiting from house to house. Soon he came to the Brailles. "What a shame," the priest thought as he watched Louis's bright face, "that such a fine mind should go untrained."

Father Palluy had an idea. Would Louis like to come to church for lessons — say three or four mornings a week?

Would he? Louis was so excited he almost forgot to say yes!

So every morning Louis tapped his way up the road to the big church on top of the hill.

On good days Louis and Father Palluy sat out in the garden. On bad days they worked inside.

Father Palluy taught Louis about history and science and how the stars move. Most often he told Louis stories from the Bible — stories of good men, bad men, brave men, and fools. Louis remembered those stories for the rest of his life.

Louis loved his lessons. But the priest was a busy man. Sometimes he didn't have time to give Louis a lesson. Also, Father Palluy wasn't trained as a teacher. And Louis was asking harder and harder questions — questions Father Palluy could not always answer.

Father Palluy had an idea. He went to see Antoine Becheret, the new school teacher of Coupvray. Could Louis become a student at his school?

Mr. Becheret had never taught a blind child before. At first he was not sure he should. After all, what good would book learning do a blind boy? It might even hurt him — make him hope for too much. Besides, maybe it was against the rules.

"But he is so hungry to learn," said the priest.

"That may be true," said the teacher. "But is it fair for him to take the place of another child — one who can see?" The school building was very small. It was really only one room.

The priest sighed. "Perhaps you are right," he said, and turned to go.

The school teacher was not sure he should take Louis. But he was also a kind man. "Wait," he said. "Don't go away with such a sad face. I've seen your little blind friend. And he *is* little. We will squeeze him in somewhere."

So after that a neighbor boy stopped by for Louis six days a week. Hand in hand they walked up the road to the little one-room schoolhouse. Going to school was very different in Louis's day. The boys sat on one side of the room, the girls on the other. The school day lasted from eight in the morning until five at night — with only a short time for lunch.

What a long day! Sometimes the other boys and girls grew restless. They wriggled or whispered or daydreamed. But Louis tried to sit as still as he could — and listen as hard as he could. He had to. He could not read. He had to listen and remember. It was the only way he could learn.

Louis's memory had always been good. Now he listened so hard that it got even better.

Louis almost never forgot what the teacher said — even months later.

Louis could also work out arithmetic problems in his head as fast as the other boys and girls could do them on paper. But when the teacher said, "All right, boys and girls, it's time to take out your books," Louis's heart sank. Then he had nothing to do.

Sometimes Louis picked up a book and ran his hands over the pages. He knew there were words on those smooth pages. But not for him! Louis was old enough to know that many of the most wonderful things in the world were written down in books. Things he would probably never learn!

Sometimes Louis thought he was going to burst with questions, spill over with all the things he wanted to know. The people around him were loving and kind. But sometimes they were too busy to answer his questions. *Wait*, they said. How tired Louis got of that word! If only he could find out things for himself. If only he could read!

There must be a way!

Father Palluy was worried about Louis. The boy was ten years old now. Soon he would be too old to go to the village school. If Louis was to continue his learning he would need a special school — a school for the blind. But were there such places?

Father Palluy began to ask questions. Soon he heard about a school in the city of Paris called The Royal Institute of Blind Youth. Could this be the place for Louis? The more Father Palluy found out, the surer he was.

The school taught all sorts of different subjects — arithmetic, grammar, geography, history, music. It also taught blind children a trade — something they could do with their hands to earn money when they grew up. But most exciting of all, the blind children were taught to *read*! Father Palluy wasn't sure how. All he knew was that they did it somehow with their hands.

He was very excited. But at first he said nothing to the Brailles. Father Palluy didn't want to get their hopes up too soon. First he wanted to make sure that the school had room for Louis.

But he was only a poor village priest. Would the school be interested in a letter from him? Father Palluy thought of a better way. He went to the richest and most powerful man in town, the Marquis d'Orvilliers. Would the Marquis write a letter to the school about Louis? Would he tell them how bright young Louis was and how eager to learn? The Marquis said he would. And before long the answer came back.

Father Palluy almost shouted for joy as he read it. For the answer was *yes*! The Institute would take Louis Braille!

Now it was time to take the good news to the Braille family. As Louis listened, a look of wild excitement grew on his face. There was a way for him to read! There was a way for him to find out things for himself!

But his mother and father did not look nearly so excited. "He is happy here," Mrs. Braille said slowly. Simon Braille nodded.

"I know," said the priest. "But Louis is growing up. Each year he grows more different from the other boys and girls. Besides, he wants so much to learn."

The Brailles both nodded. They knew all of this was true. But they were still worried. They wanted what was best for Louis. But they were afraid too. The city of Paris was thirty miles from Coupvray. Louis would have to stay there for months. He would be able to come home only for summer vacations. Their son was just ten years old — and blind. Could he get along in the big city without their help?

Louis had no doubts at all. All *he* could think of were those books. All kinds of books for him to read by himself! He touched his way across the room. "Papa," he begged. *"Please."*

New Boy

STILL Simon Braille didn't say *yes* or *no* — not right away. First he wrote to the Institute. He had many questions to ask. The answers must have pleased him. For finally he said yes! And so one cold day in February, 1819, Louis climbed on a stagecoach and rode off to school.

But school wasn't at all what Louis had hoped it would be — not at first.

The first day was almost like a nightmare of too many people and too much noise. Nearly one hundred blind students went to the Institute. Louis was introduced to one after another. He tried to keep their names straight. But they just jumbled together in his head. Louis had never been with so many boys before. And he had never felt more alone.

Finally the long day was over. Louis lay for the first time in his narrow school bed — in the middle of a long line of other beds. He was tired. But he could not sleep. He had a strange feeling — as if he had swallowed something cold and hard.

Ten-year-old Louis had never been away from home before. He didn't know he was homesick. But he did know he was miserable. Finally he buried his head in the pillow and began to cry.

"Don't cry . . ." A voice from the next bed spoke. "Here." Louis felt a handkerchief being put in his hand.

"Go on. Blow," the friendly voice went on. "There! Doesn't that feel better?"

The voice was closer now. Louis felt his bed sink as someone sat on it. "My name's Gabriel. Gabriel Gautier. What's yours?"

"Louis . . . Louis Braille," Louis said between sobs.

"Listen, Louis," Gabriel said. "You've just got the new-boy blues. Everyone gets them at first. I did too."

"You . . . you did?"

"Yes. But they go away. So go to sleep now. You'll feel better tomorrow. Wait and see.

"Good night," Gabriel said softly — back in his own bed again.

"Night . . ." Louis wriggled down under the covers. He even smiled a little. For he did feel better. He had made his first friend.

Louis needed a friend in the next few weeks. There were so many strange things to get used to. Louis was a country boy. He was used to sunshine and plenty of fresh air. Everything seemed so crowded and dirty to him here in the city. He was used to being clean. In the summer Louis had bathed almost every day in the nearby creek. In the winter his mother kept a big pot of water hot over the fire. But here at the Institute there was only one bathroom for all of the boys. They were allowed to take only one bath a month!

And the old school building was so big. Halls went off in every direction. There were staircases everywhere. Louis had lived all his life in a two-room house. He got lost again and again. Would he ever find his way around this big old barn of a place?

But what bothered Louis most of all was the dampness. The school building was built very close to a river. So inside, the air was always cold and wet. When Louis first came to the Institute his cheeks were rosy with health. But soon he was as pale as the rest of the boys. Many of them had hacking coughs that would not go away. A visiting doctor said the damp air was bad for their lungs.

So at first all Louis could think of was his family and his home in Coupvray. But bit by bit things got better. Louis got used to the school and the strange city ways. He learned to get around the big old building. He began to make friends with more and more boys. And before long he was simply too busy to be homesick or sad. He had classes from morning to night.

Grammar, geography, history, arithmetic, music — Louis loved them all. Ten-year-old Louis Braille was the youngest boy in school. But right from the beginning he was often at the head of his class. "This boy is gifted with great ease of learning," a teacher wrote. "You almost never have to tell him something twice."

Every afternoon the boys tap-touched their way down the halls to one of the workshops. There they knitted caps and mittens, made straw and leather slippers, or wove long rawhide whips for cattle and oxen. Louis had helped his father in the harness shop for years. It had been good training. From the beginning he was good with his hands. At the end of the first year Louis even won a special prize for knitting and slipper making.

But Louis's favorite time of day was late afternoon. Then he went to music class. All the boys learned to play some musical instrument. Louis learned to play several. But from the beginning he showed a special talent for the piano. Louis loved to press the keys and hear the sounds — happy or sad. Music was going to be one of the great joys of Louis Braille's life.

The blind boys could not wander the crowded streets of Paris alone. So most of the time they had to stay inside. But every Thursday they were taken for a special walk. It wasn't easy to take so many blind boys through the busy streets of Paris. But the school worked out a way. A teacher held the end of a long rope. The blind boys lined up behind, each holding onto the rope. When the teacher started to walk, the rest of the rope followed after — wriggling like a snake — a snake with many legs!

The boys knew they probably looked funny. But they just laughed and called themselves "the rope gang" — and held their heads high.

At first the busy city streets scared Louis.

They were so different from the quiet country roads of home. Bells ringing, boats tooting, carts and wagons rumbling through every alley and street. It was too much noise!

And the people! There were so many of them — pushing, shoving, rushing by. Why was everyone in such a hurry? Louis wondered. People never rushed like this at home.

But soon Louis began to sort out the sounds of the city. He learned to tell the churches of Paris apart by the different sounds of their bells — and the boats on the nearby river by their whistles. A loud *crunch-crunch* sound on a cobblestone street was a soldier's boots passing by. And a certain *swish-swish* sound meant a lady's long silk skirt. Louis already knew the sounds of country birds. Now he also learned the *whurr* of pigeons' wings. And the scratchy sound of their feet on the hard city streets.

"It's Just a Show-off Trick!"

So the busy months passed. And Louis grew happier and happier with his life at school. Only one thing was wrong — but it was the most important thing of all.

Louis was taking reading lessons. But it wasn't anything like what he had dreamed of for so long. In 1820 there was only one way for the blind to read. It was called *raised-print*. Each letter of the alphabet was raised from the page. It stood up from the paper background so it could be felt with the fingers. This sounded easy. But it wasn't.

Some of the letters were simple to feel. But

others were almost impossible to tell apart. The *Q*'s felt like *O*'s. The *O*'s felt like *C*'s. The *I*'s turned out to be *T*'s and the *R*'s were really *B*'s.

But Louis was determined. Again and again his fingers traced the raised letters until he could tell them apart — most of the time. Then letter by letter he began to feel out words.

But it was so slow! Louis was one of the brightest boys in the school. But often even he forgot the beginning of a sentence before he got to the end of it. Then he had to go back the whole way and start over again.

It would take months to read a single book this way! "This isn't really reading," Louis cried one day. "It's just a show-off trick!"

"It's the best we can do," a teacher answered. "People have tried to find a better way for years."

Louis knew this was true. He knew that people had tried so many things — raised letters, lowered letters, letters of stone and letters of string, letters of wax and letters of wood. One man had even made an alphabet of pins. Louis tried to imagine how it would feel to read a page of pins. Ouch!

Besides, Louis soon learned that in the entire school library there were just fourteen books. Just fourteen! And there were good reasons for this. The raised-print books were very expensive to make. Each one had to be made by hand. They were also big and hard to store. Each letter had to be at least three inches from top to bottom — or blind fingers could not feel it. So only a few words could fit on a page.

No. Louis knew now that there would never be many books for the blind. Not the raised-print way. Then there must be another, better way! There just had to be! Soon that was all Louis could think — or talk — about. And his friends got good and tired of it.

"Do shut up, Louis," they begged.

"But it's so important!" Louis tried to explain. "Don't you see? Without books we can never really learn! But just think what we could grow up to be if only we could read. Doctors or lawyers or scientists. Or writers even! *Anything* almost."

"All right," one of the boys snapped. "We want to read too. Find us a way, if you're so smart."

"I can't," Louis cried. "I'm blind!"

Then one day in the spring of 1821 Captain Charles Barbier came to the Institute. Captain Barbier had worked out a way for his soldiers to send messages to each other in the dark. He called it nightwriting. The Captain thought it might work for the blind too.

Nightwriting used raised dots. A word was broken down into sounds. Each sound was given a different pattern of raised dots. The dots were pushed — or punched — into heavy sheets of paper with a long pointed tool called a *stylus*. When the paper was turned over, raised dots could be felt on the other side.

Dots! At first the blind boys were very

excited. There were so many things right about dots! They were so small — just feel how many fit under a single fingertip. And they were so easy to feel!

But before long the boys knew that many things were wrong with Captain Barbier's nightwriting, too. There were so many things it would not do. There was no way to make capital letters or write numbers. There was no way to make periods or commas or exclamation points. It took up far too much room. But most of all it was so hard to learn and hard to feel.

Nightwriting might work well enough for soldiers to send simple notes like "advance" or "enemy is behind you." But it was no way to read or write many words. It was no way to make many books for the blind.

So nightwriting was a failure. Did that mean dots were a failure too? Louis didn't think so. As the days passed it was all he could think of. He even dreamed of dots at night.

And before long Louis made up his mind.

He was going to do it himself. He was going to work out a way for the blind to *really* read and write with dots! Quickly and easily. At least he was going to try with all his heart and mind.

Louis set right to work. He was almost never without his tools now. Wherever he went he took heavy sheets of paper, a board to rest them on, and his stylus — the long, thin tool for punching dots. (The stylus was shaped almost exactly like an *awl* — the tool that had made Louis blind.)

Captain Barbier soon heard that someone was trying to make his nightwriting better. He hurried to the Institute to see who it was.

Louis was excited when he learned he was

going to meet Captain Barbier, the man who had invented nightwriting. It was Captain Barbier who had worked with dots in the first place! Would the Captain like his ideas? Louis hoped so!

But things went wrong from the start. Captain Barbier's eyebrows rose with surprise as Louis tapped into the room. He had been expecting a man. Not a twelve-year-old boy! Louis couldn't see the look on Captain Barbier's face. But he could hear the chill in his voice.

"I hear you think you have worked out some improvements on my system," the Captain said.

"Yes . . . yes, sir," Louis answered.

"Well?"

"Sir . . . ?" said Louis, confused.

"Explain, explain!"

Louis tried. But the more he talked, the more he could tell that Captain Barbier wasn't really listening.

But Louis kept trying. "S . . . sir. One thing that must be worked out. We must find a

way for words to . . . to be spelled the same
way again and again."

"Why?" said the Captain. His voice was
cold as ice.

"So . . . so we can have books — many
books."

"Why?" the Captain asked again. Captain
Barbier was like many other people in
Louis's day. He felt sorry for blind people.
He would never be cruel to them. But he did

not think they were as smart as other people — people who could see. He thought blind people should be satisfied with simple things — like being able to read short notes and signs and directions. He certainly didn't think they needed many books!

"Is that all?" said the Captain.

"Yes . . ." Louis was almost whispering now.

"Very interesting," Captain Barbier snapped. "I will think about it." But Louis knew he would not. Captain Barbier was a proud man — too proud. He was used to giving orders and having them obeyed. He might have been able to accept these ideas from another man. But from a boy? A half-grown child? No, he didn't like it. He didn't like it at all!

Captain Barbier said a few more stiff words. Then with a bang of the door he was gone.

Louis sighed. He knew he would get no help from the Captain. He would have to work alone.

The Alphabet of Dots

Louis tried not to waste a single minute. Even when he was home on vacation, he worked on his dots. Often his mother would pack him a lunch of bread and cheese and fruit, and he would wander out to sit on some sunny hillside. Other times he sat by the side of the road, bent over his paper and board. "There is Louis, making his pinpricks," the neighbors said with a smile as they passed. What was he doing? Was it some kind of a game the blind boy was playing to keep himself busy? Louis didn't try to explain. He just went on punching patterns of dots.

At home in Coupvray Louis had plenty of free time to work on his experiments. At school it was not nearly so easy. There were so many other things to do. Louis had to go to class. He had to spend an hour or two in one of the workshops every day. He had to practice his music and do his homework. He had to eat meals with the rest of the boys — or someone would come looking for him.

But Louis still found time to work on his ideas. He worked in bits and pieces. He worked before breakfast. And between classes. He worked after dinner. And late at night.

That was the best time of all. The boys were all asleep, and everything was quiet. Hour after hour Louis bent over his board, experimenting with different patterns of dots.

Sometimes he got so tired he fell asleep sitting up. Sometimes he became so excited he forgot what time it was and worked until he heard the milk wagons rattling by under his window. Louis would raise his head with surprise then. For he knew it was early morning. He had worked the whole night through again! Then Louis would crawl into bed to nap for an hour or two — before he had to get up yawning for breakfast and his first class.

Louis's friends became more and more worried about him.

"You never sleep!"

"Half the time you forget to eat!"

"And for what?" a third boy snapped. "A wild goose chase! That's what!"

"Maybe you're right," Louis always answered them softly. And he kept on working.

Three years went by — three years of hard work and trying and not quite succeeding.

Sometimes Louis got so tired he could hardly lift his hand. And sometimes he became very, very discouraged.

Again and again Louis had simplified Captain Barbier's patterns of dots. But still they were not simple enough. No, reading with dots was still too hard.

Were the boys right? Was this a wild goose chase? Men had been working on this problem for hundreds of years — smart men, important men, older men. And one after another *they* had failed. Who did he think he was? What right did he have to think he could do better than they? "Sometimes I think I'll kill myself if I don't succeed," Louis said to Gabriel.

Then Louis had a new and very different idea. It seemed so simple — after he'd had it. Captain Barbier's nightwriting had been based on *sounds*. But there were so many sounds in the French language. Sometimes it took almost a hundred dots to write out a simple word. This was far, far too many to feel easily with the fingertips. But what if he used dots in a different way? What if the patterns of dots didn't stand for sounds at all? What if they stood for the letters of the alphabet instead? There were only twenty-six of them, after all!

Louis was filled with excitement. He was sure he was right! Now he worked even harder. And everything began to fall into place.

First Louis took a pencil and marked six dots on a heavy piece of paper. He called this six-dot pattern a *cell*. It looked like this:

o   o

o   o

o   o

He numbered each dot in the cell:

1 o   o 4

2 o   o 5

3 o   o 6

Then he took his stylus and raised dot number one — that would stand for *A*:

●   o

o   o

o   o

He raised dots number one and two — and that would stand for *B*:

●   o

●   o

o   o

Raised dots number one and four would be *C*:

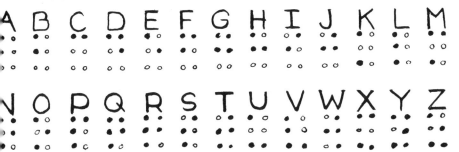

Louis made letter after letter. And when he was finished Louis Braille's alphabet of dots looked like this:

Louis ran his fingers over his alphabet. It was so simple! So simple! Fifteen-year-old Louis Braille felt like shouting or crying or laughing out loud. All the letters of the alphabet had been made out of the same six dots — used over and over again in different patterns! He knew it wouldn't look like much of anything to people who could see. But it wasn't supposed to! It was meant to be felt! Quickly. Easily. And it worked!

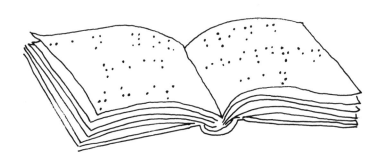

So Many Ways to Say No

L ouis was home in Coupvray when he finished his alphabet. He could hardly wait to get back to school and show it to the other boys. What would they say? Would they like it? They just had to!

Louis wasn't disappointed. The boys loved his alphabet from first touch.

"It's so simple!"

"So easy to feel."

"And so small — so much fits right under my fingertips."

"We can write! We can write letters to each other!"

"And keep diaries!"

"We can take notes in class . . ."

"And read them back later!"

"And books," Louis said quietly. "Don't forget about books. Soon we will have all sorts — just for us to read."

News of the alphabet spread quickly through the school. Soon the director of the Institute sent for Louis.

"Tell me," Dr. Pignier said. "What is this . . . this alphabet of dots I've been hearing so much about?"

"Please, sir," answered Louis eagerly. "If you will read something aloud, I'll show you."

So Dr. Pignier picked up a book and began to read — slowly.

"You can go faster, sir," said Louis. Soon Louis's hand was flying across the paper — punching words into dots. When the director stopped reading, Louis turned the paper over. He brushed his fingers lightly over the lines of raised dots. Then quickly, easily — without a single mistake — he read back every word.

"Amazing," Dr. Pignier kept murmuring. "Amazing. . . . How old are you, my boy?"

"Fifteen," Louis answered.

"Fifteen! To think that men have been searching for just such an alphabet for hundreds of years — and one of *my* boys has found it instead. Fifteen. Amazing!"

Louis glowed with pride. Now was the time to ask the most important question of all. "Sir, when can we start making books?"

Dr. Pignier was silent for a long time. *What was wrong?* Finally he spoke. "You are young, Louis," he said.

Louis frowned. What kind of an answer was this? Dr. Pignier tried to explain. The Institute was a charity school — it had no money of its own. Some of the money it needed came from the government, some from rich friends. But there was no money left over to make books

"Sir," Louis said. "Will you write to these men — these men who have money? Will you

tell them how my alphabet works? Will you tell them how cheaply it can be made into books?"

"I will," said Dr. Pignier. "But Louis, don't get your hopes up too high. Some things take time — a great deal of time."

Dr. Pignier sat down and wrote letter after letter. He wrote to rich men. He wrote to important men. He wrote to men who had spent their whole lives working for the blind. One by one their answers came back.

Some were long. Some were short. Some were written with fancy words. But they all ended up saying exactly the same thing in the end — *no*.

Some people just didn't like change of any sort. "What's wrong with the old ways?" they wrote. "They've worked well enough all these years."

One man had already given money to help make some of the old raised-print books. "Now you tell me they are not good enough," he wrote angrily. "Well, let me tell you something. They had better be. You will not get another cent from me!"

A few people were even jealous. One man who ran another school for the blind, wrote: "I will allow this to be tried out in my school — *over my dead body!*" He was afraid Louis's alphabet might be too good. He was working on one of his own!

And many, many people didn't say *no* — or *yes*. "This sounds very interesting," one man wrote. "I'll get to it as soon as I can." But when would that be? Next week? Next month? Or never? People like this weren't against Louis's alphabet. They just didn't care. They were too busy with their own lives to bother with the problems of the blind.

So the years began to pass. And nothing much happened. The blind students kept on using Louis's alphabet. But there were only a hundred students. What about the millions and millions of blind people all over the world — still waiting for books? Louis couldn't get them out of his mind.

He tried to stay cheerful. But it wasn't always easy. Sometimes his mind filled with bitter thoughts. His alphabet was good. He had proved that! But no one cared. Not enough.

More than three years passed. When Louis was nineteen he graduated from the Institute. But he didn't leave the school.

Dr. Pignier had been watching Louis for years now. He had seen him grow from a boy to a man. Every year Louis Braille won a prize in something — grammar, history, geography, arithmetic, piano, even working with his hands. Dr. Pignier knew that Louis was also a natural leader. He loved to joke and tell stories. Just as important, he knew how to listen quietly when other people had troubles to tell.

Yes, Dr. Pignier decided, Louis would be too good to lose. So now he asked him to stay on at the Institute as a teacher.

A teacher! Louis accepted joyfully. For more than anything he wanted to stay in Paris. Paris was where the people were — people who could help him with his alphabet. If only they would. Besides, Louis had grown to love the school and his many friends there. It was like a second home to him now.

Dr. Pignier warned Louis that the pay wouldn't be much — only fifteen francs a month. But as a teacher, Louis would have the right to leave the school building any time he wanted without asking permission. And for the first time in his life he had a

room of his own. It took Louis quite a while to get used to the silence!

Louis liked teaching. He was good at it, too. For one thing he always spent a lot of time getting his lessons ready for class. Every night he sat at his desk and thought about what he wanted to say the next day. Then he punched his thoughts in dots. So he never stuttered or stumbled or forgot what he wanted to say. From the beginning everyone looked up to Louis Braille as a teacher. And they trusted him as a friend.

School teachers were not supposed to be kind and patient in Louis's day. Many of them were not. They shouted and yelled and made fun of slow boys. They thought learning was something that had to be pounded into children's heads.

Louis knew this was wrong. "He used a firm kindness instead," a friend later wrote. Louis never made fun of his students — no matter how slow or silly they were being. And he was especially gentle with the youngest boys. Louis had been at the school for many years now. But he had never forgotten what it felt like to be new and shy and alone!

Louis loved his life as a teacher. But as usual, he was working too hard. He taught many different classes. He spent a lot of time with his friends. He was never too busy to help a boy with his work. Or to listen to someone else's troubles.

Every day he practiced his music for several hours. Ever since Louis had come to the Institute he had played the piano — and then the organ. Now he was very, very good. In 1833 he was made organist at Saint Nicholas-des-Champs, one of the biggest churches in Paris. People were beginning to say that Louis could be really famous one day — if he would forget everything else and work most of the time on his music.

Louis loved music. It stirred such big feelings inside of him. It would always be a very important part of his life. But something else was more important — the alphabet of dots.

Louis was working on a way to make patterns of dots stand for musical notes — and for numbers too. He also spent a great deal of time making raised-dot books for the school library. Friends who could see sometimes helped him by reading the words aloud.

It was slow, hard work. Hour after hour, night after night, Louis sat up punching dots. He worked until his back ached and his fingers grew stiff and sore.

Louis could not keep on working this hard forever. First came a tiredness. Some days he could hardly drag himself from bed. But at first he tried to fool himself. "All I need is a good night's sleep," he told himself again and again. "I'll feel better in the morning." But most often he felt worse instead.

Some days he could not even climb a flight of stairs without stopping to rest. The boys in his class had to lean forward in their chairs to hear him — his voice was so weak.

One day his head would be hot with fever. The next day his whole body would shake with chills. But worst of all was the cough. It grew worse and worse.

One morning Louis coughed so hard he
could not get out of bed. The doctor
came — and shook his head at the sounds he
heard. For a long time the doctor stood
silent. He didn't want to say what he knew
he had to say. Finally he asked, "Do you
know what is wrong with you?"

"Yes," Louis whispered. For he had stopped trying to fool himself by now. Louis Braille was no doctor. But he knew the signs. Besides, other people at the Institute had suffered from the same sickness because the air was so damp. He had tuberculosis — a disease of the lungs.

"Some people say fresh air helps," the doctor said. "And plenty of rest."

But Louis and the doctor both knew that there was no real cure for tuberculosis — not then. It came and went — but it always came again.

Louis lay still for hours after the doctor left. He felt too sad to move. Why did this have to happen to him? He was only twenty-six years old! He didn't want to die! And what would happen to his alphabet?

Finally Louis made a decision. He had been a fighter all his life. He would not let this terrible disease beat him so easily now. He might not have a long life. But he would have a full one!

Troubles

Louis followed the doctor's orders. He slept long hours each day. He ate everything that was put in front of him. As soon as he was a little stronger he spent some time every day out in the fresh air. And slowly he grew stronger again. Not as strong as before. But strong enough.

Finally Louis felt well enough to begin teaching again. The time passed. And Louis was happy with much of his life — his teaching, his music, his friends. But things did not go so well with his alphabet.

Luckily Louis did not have to carry on the fight completely alone. The director of the

Institute continued to be a good friend. He was always willing to help.

Dr. Pignier saved for a long time. Finally he had enough money set aside to print a small book about Louis's alphabet. The two of them worked and worried over each page. They wanted it to be just right. Finally they were finished. Louis was so proud. He decided to call the book, *Method of Writing Words, Music, and Plain-song by Means of Dots for Use by the Blind and Arranged by Them.* What a long, important sounding title! Surely such an important sounding book would find friends for his alphabet somewhere.

Dr. Pignier sent copies to many important men. But the months passed. And all he and Louis got back were polite thank-you notes. Or nothing at all.

One day Louis was riding home to Coupvray in a stagecoach. He was going to visit his parents. Before long he discovered that a blind woman was riding with him. Louis spent the next few hours telling her about the alphabet. And showing her how to feel the raised dots. The blind woman was very excited. Blind people almost always were.

"Then teach others," Louis said.

"I will," she promised. But did she? Louis never knew.

Louis didn't like to talk to strangers. But in the next few years he talked to many. He talked to anyone who could help him, if only they would! At night, when he couldn't sleep, Louis would sometimes remember their words.

"You are young, Mr. Braille . . ."

"Everything takes time, Mr. Braille . . ."

"You must understand, Mr. Braille . . ."

"You must be patient, Mr. Braille . . ."

Patient! Louis felt like shouting when people talked like this! He didn't have *time* to be patient! He was only in his early thirties. He was still a young man. But he had been sick for years with tuberculosis. And each year he had grown weaker. How much time did he have left?

Then came the worst blow of all. Louis had faced many disappointments in the past few years. But he was always sure his alphabet would be welcomed in one place — the Institute itself. After all, the director was one of his closest friends. But in 1841 Dr. Pignier left the Institute. A new man took his place.

The new director, Dr. Dufau, was a very different man from Dr. Pignier. Dr. Dufau was stern and cold. He did not like to take chances. He did not like anything new or different. So of course he did not like Louis's alphabet. "That silly punching of dots!" he called it more than once. But at first he let the boys go on using Louis's alphabet.

Then Louis fell ill once again. Day after day he lay coughing in bed. It was winter in Paris, and very cold and damp. When the doctor examined Louis, his words were sharp. "If you stay here, Mr. Braille, you will be dead within weeks."

There was only one thing to do. Louis's friends packed his bags. He was going home to Coupvray again — not for a vacation — but to fight for his life.

"I'll be back soon," Louis said as cheerfully as he could. But his friends could hardly hold back their tears. They were sure they were saying good-by forever.

But once more Louis surprised everyone. Somehow he got better again. It took a long time. Six months passed before Louis felt strong enough to return to Paris. He could hardly wait to be with his old friends and students, and start to work again.

But as soon as Louis got back to school, he knew something was wrong. His friends were too silent. His students talked about everything except one thing.

"What's wrong?" Louis asked.

Finally they told him. Dr. Dufau had grown bolder and bolder with Louis gone. First he had said the boys could not use the alphabet in class. Then he said they could not use it anywhere. "Not even in our room," one boy said softly.

Only one more question had to be asked. "What about my books?"

Everyone knew Louis was talking about the raised-dot books he had worked so many days and nights to make for the school library. There was a long silence.

"He burned them."

"All?"

"Every one."

Louis shook his head. "All my books . . . gone." He turned and touched his way from the room.

The next few weeks were the worst of Louis's life. He taught his classes. He ate. He slept. But it was as if he were living in a dream — a bad dream.

Louis's body was worn out. Now so was his spirit. He knew that he could not fight this impossible fight any longer.

Luckily he didn't have to. The blind boys fought it for him. The alphabet was forbidden. But they simply refused to give it up. Dr. Dufau took away their tools — the heavy paper and every stylus he could find. But the boys just found substitutes — darning needles, knitting needles, even nails — and went right on using Louis's alphabet.

The older boys taught new boys in secret

late at night. Everyone kept a hidden diary and passed secret notes. The boys knew they would be punished if they were caught. They were sent to their rooms without food. They were hit across the hands. But still they would not stop.

Many of the teachers who could see agreed with Dr. Dufau. They didn't like Louis's alphabet either. Some were just lazy. They already knew how to read with their eyes. Why should they bother to learn another way? But most were afraid. What if this raised-dot alphabet really caught on? What if a great many books were printed in it? Then this school — and others like it — could be run by blind teachers entirely. What would happen then to their jobs?

Luckily one teacher did not agree. Dr. Joseph Gaudet was new to the school. He watched this battle between the director and the boys. And the more he watched, the more he came to like the alphabet. "You can order the boys not to use it," he said to Dr. Dufau. "But I think the day will come when blind people everywhere will be using Braille's dots."

Dr. Dufau listened. He was getting awfully tired of this fight with the boys — this fight he could not seem to win!

". . . and if it catches on," Gaudet continued, "wouldn't you like to be known as the man who helped it in the beginning?"

That sounded good! Dr. Dufau was an ambitious man — he loved being on the winning side of things. Besides, he was learning something the hard way. He was learning that he could burn a book — he could forbid a whole system — but it was much, much harder to stop a boy from thinking. Or to make him forget something he wanted to remember.

So Dr. Dufau changed his mind completely. He gave new orders. From now on the blind boys could use Louis's alphabet once more. Anywhere. Anytime.

And that wasn't all.

A Demonstration of Dots

THE old school building was dirty and cramped. For years it had been on the edge of tumbling down. Finally money was found to build a new building and in 1844 the Institute moved.

Dr. Dufau planned the opening day ceremonies carefully. Many important people had been asked to attend — teachers and scientists and government officials. There would be speeches, of course. But the best part of the ceremonies would be an explanation — an explanation of Louis Braille's dots!

Louis sat with the other teachers high up

on the stage. He slipped into his seat just as the ceremonies began. He could hear the audience turning and twisting in their chairs.

First came the speeches. Most were long and dull. The audience began to make whispering noises. "Hurry!" Louis thought.

Finally his turn came. First Joseph Gaudet stood and read a paper explaining the alphabet. People were still moving in their chairs and whispering. Then Dr. Dufau led a blind girl to the front of the stage. She had big brown eyes and long curly hair. The audience grew quieter. Already this was better than any speech!

Dr. Dufau opened a book and began to read. The little girl stood by his side and wrote down his words in Louis Braille's dots. When Dr. Dufau finished reading he touched the child on the shoulder. Quickly she skimmed her fingertips over the rows of dots she'd just made. Then word for word she spoke them back.

The audience was very impressed! Many rose to their feet to clap. But a few refused to

believe their ears. It seemed impossible to them.

"It's a trick!" a voice yelled from the audience.

"Yes! She learned it before!"

A trick? The clapping slowed. But before it could stop altogether Louis jumped to his feet. He touched his way over to Dr. Dufau and whispered in his ear. Dr. Dufau listened hard for a few moments. Then he nodded and rose.

He spread his hands wide. "Wait, my friends, wait!" he called in a loud voice. "Give me a few minutes. And I will prove that what you have seen is no trick."

Slowly the audience grew quiet again.

Louis let out a sigh of relief. They would wait — for a while.

Quickly Dr. Dufau called up two blind children. He sent one child from the room. The other he kept by his side.

"Now," Dr. Dufau spoke to the audience. "Will someone please come up onto the stage? Anyone at all will do."

A man finally came forward. Dr. Dufau held out a pile of books. "Please pick any one," he said. "And turn to whatever page you wish. Read anything you like."

As the man read, the blind child wrote the words down in dots. Then the other child was led back into the room. Dr. Dufau gave him the newly made page of dots. "Please read what is written there," he said. The child nodded. His fingers brushed lightly across the page of dots. Then loudly, clearly, he spoke them word for word.

There could be no doubt this time! The audience stood up and cheered.

Louis felt like shouting for joy! The first big step had been taken! At last.

One by One the Last Years Pass

So the worst of the fight was over. And just in time. Louis had lived for so many years with tuberculosis — sometimes very sick, sometimes almost well. Now he felt very weak once more. "I'll feel better soon," Louis told himself. He always had before. But this time was different.

In 1844 Louis's days as a classroom teacher came to an end. He was only thirty-five years old. But from now on he had to spend most of his time in bed. He had to leave the fight for his alphabet to other, stronger men.

But Louis still followed news of it. And for the first time some of the news was good. More and more letters were being written to the Institute asking for information about the raised-dot alphabet. (People were beginning to call it *braille*. Louis liked that!)

A few teachers were beginning to try the alphabet out in other schools for the blind. In 1847 the first braille printing press was made. Now raised-dot books could be made by machine, instead of the old, slow way, by hand.

So one by one the last years passed. Louis had to live quietly now. When he felt well enough he gave a few piano lessons to the boys. Other times he worked in bed, punching patterns of dots, making one book after another for the school library. And he continued to work and dream of new and better ways to use the alphabet.

Louis's room was often crowded with friends who had come to see him. It rang with laughter and good talk. Louis Braille might be weak and bedridden. But he was

still one of the most popular men at school.

"He would have sacrificed everything for any one of us," a friend later wrote, "his time, his health, everything he owned."

Louis never talked about all the giving he did. "He never wanted to be thanked," another friend said later. But on the back of his desk was a small black box. Inside it was stuffed to the brim with slips of paper. They were I-O-U's — promises people had made to pay back money to Louis Braille. In Louis's will he wrote, "Destroy the box when I die."

One damp, cold day in December, 1851, Louis caught a cold. It was just a cold. But he was so weak, he could not get over it. His fever climbed higher and higher. His old cough grew worse and worse.

All Louis's friends came to see him. They tried to tell him he was getting better. But Louis only shook his head. He knew — he'd been close to death so many times. "You don't have to pretend with me," he said softly now.

Louis was not afraid of death. A priest came to pray with him and prepare him for it. Louis said after the priest's visit, "I tasted the greatest of joys." But Louis Braille loved life too. He also said, "I asked God to take me from the world, it is true. But I felt I wasn't asking very hard!"

But Louis's life was almost over all the same. On January 6, 1852, it rained all day. The wind howled around the building. Hour after hour the storm grew worse. Thunder and lightning filled the air. It sounded like giants battling outside. Louis turned his face to the window and smiled. He had always liked a good fight. Then he closed his eyes for the last time.

Louis Braille was dead. His many friends missed him and were very sad. But he was not a well-known man. Not one newspaper in all of Paris printed the news of his death. Yet today his name is known all around the world. He was a simple school teacher. He never made much money. Yet today blind people everywhere bless him for giving them one of the greatest gifts of all time — the alphabet called braille.

Finally Louis's alphabet began to catch on. Slowly at first, then faster and faster. No blind boy or girl who learned braille ever forgot the feel of those dots. They helped spread the word. More and more books were coming from the braille printing presses. The braille alphabet was being translated into many different languages — even Chinese!

Six years after Louis Braille died, the first school for the blind in America began to use his alphabet. In another thirty years, almost every school for the blind in Europe had changed to it!

In 1887, the people of Coupvray, where Louis was born, built a monument to him in the middle of the village square. On one side

of the tall marble column was the alphabet of dots, and the words: "To Braille from the Grateful Blind." On the other side was a raised picture of Louis teaching a blind child to read with his hands. The statue is still there today in the middle of the same village square where blind Louis played as a boy. Today everyone proudly calls the square "La Place Braille."

Louis's name became known around the world. Schools were named after him, and magazines too. He was mentioned in encyclopedias, his face was put on a special issue of stamps. Statues and monuments were raised to him in many countries. But the best monuments of all were the special libraries full of books — braille books for the blind!

When Louis died in 1852, not one newspaper in all of Paris wrote of his death. In 1952, a hundred years later, newspapers everywhere had stories about him. Louis's body had been buried in the little country cemetery of Coupvray. Now his coffin was taken from there and carried to Paris. From now on it would rest in a building called the Pantheon — the burial place of France's most honored men. Over the main door of the building were the words: "To its Greatest Men — the Country Gives Honor." Now France — and the world — were honoring Louis Braille.

First there was a solemn march. A band played a slow tune. All across the city of Paris church bells rang out as Louis's coffin was carried through the streets.

Behind it walked many of the world's most famous people. The President of France was there. Helen Keller was too. But behind these important people came the ones who had always mattered most to Louis — row after row of unknown blind, tapping their white-tipped canes. They were there to say thank you once more to Louis Braille — who had filled so much of the emptiness in their lives with books.

FINIS

About the author

MARGARET DAVIDSON was born in New York City. She is a well-known author of children's books, particularly noted for her biographies. She has written about Frederick Douglass, Thomas Edison, Eleanor Roosevelt and George Washington. Besides *Louis Braille*, she has written two other biographies dealing with blindness — *Helen Keller* (Hastings House) and *Helen Keller's Teacher* (Four Winds) which was the winner of the 1967 Junior Book Award.

Always striving for maximum authenticity, Mrs. Davidson found researching *Louis Braille* a particularly difficult task. Having exhausted all the books in English on the subject, she also tracked down French sources (including 19th century documents) for the most accurate information available.

Mrs. Davidson lives with her husband, a filmmaker, in New York City.

About the artist

Besides illustrating children's books, Janet Compere is also an artist of some renown. Her work can be seen in the permanent collections of the Whitney Museum and the Brooklyn Museum. A native New Yorker, Miss Compere graduated from Baylor University where she majored in drama.

10/81

CHESTERFIELD COUNTY LIBRARY
ETTRICK-MATOACA

Regular loan: 2 weeks
A daily fine is charged for each overdue book.
Books may be renewed once, unless reserved for
another patron.
A borrower is responsible for books damaged
or lost while charged on his card.